Machines at work
DIGGER

SANDY CREEK

Written and edited by Nicola Deschamps
Designed by Susan Calver
Additional design Helen Chapman,
Jacqueline Gooden, and Cheryl Telfer
Publishing Manager Susan Leonard
Managing art editor Clare Shedden
Jacket design Bob Warner
Picture researcher Sarah Stewart-Richardson
Production Janet Levesley
DTP Designer Almudena Díaz
Consultant J. Bowles

Sandy Creek
122 Fifth Avenue
New York, NY 10011

ISBN: 978-1-4351-1562-0

A Cataloging-in-Publication record for this book
is available from the Library of Congress.

Color reproduction by Media, Development and Printing Ltd., U.K.
Printed and bound in China by Toppan Printing Co., Ltd.

3 5 7 9 10 8 6 4 2

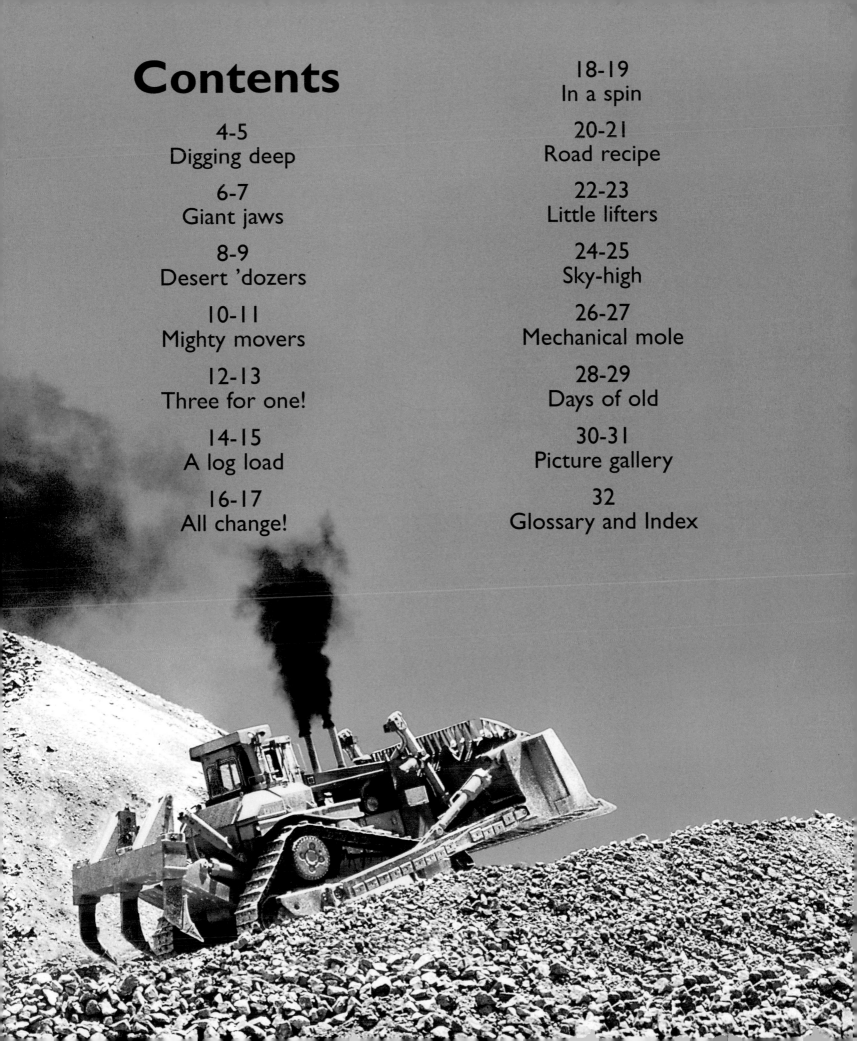

Contents

Digging deep

Excavators come in all shapes and sizes, and there are some that run on **tracks**, while others have **wheels.**

This excavator can run over uneven ground easily and safely on these wide crawler tracks.

VOLVO

Creeping crawlers
A crawler track is made up of lots of separate pieces that fit together to form a flexible band, which is driven by sprockets or wheels.

This big excavator can dig and lift over 14 tons (13 metric tons) of rubble. That's as heavy as three elephants!

Big bucket

This excavator is using a bucket attachment that has sharp teeth. These help it to cut through soil and rubble.

Stick

Boom

Wheelies

This little wheeled excavator can run almost as fast as a car, so it can be easily transported from one site to another. The boom and stick can be safely folded away while on the road.

It's a fact

The Komatsu PCO1 is a tiny excavator; it's the size of a motorcycle!

A giant mining excavator is so big that the operator has to climb up a stepladder to reach the cab!

Giant jaws

This mighty machine works in the **demolition** industry and can rip apart a house in just two hours! It bites into buildings, demolishing them bit by bit.

This muncher attachment can tear down steel structures and crush concrete floors.

Crunch!

Munch!

Boom!

Explosives are used mostly to demolish high-rise buildings— a 20-story building can be destroyed in just four seconds!

An articulated arm can reach up to 138 feet (42 meters), which is taller than a 10-story building.

Old methods

The earliest demolition tool was a wrecking ball, which was used to smash down buildings. It was swung against the side of a building again and again until the building fell down.

Wrecking ball

High-spy

Some long-reach excavators have a camera attached to the top of the arm, which allows the driver to see what the muncher is doing.

A heavy weight, called a counterbalance, stops this machine from tipping over.

Desert 'dozers

Using their huge metal **blades**, bulldozers can **push** and **cut** their way through anything in their path, even a desert!

These bulldozers are helping to clear sand to make way for canal-building.

Up and down
The driver can tilt this bulldozer's blade downward to cut and push, or upward to build up a big pile.

Pulling power
With a blade to push aside snow, tracks to grip, and a powerful engine, this bulldozer is ideal for pulling vehicles through the snow.

Rip it up
The sharp prongs at the back of this bulldozer make up the ripper attachment. This is used to tear up the ground for leveling or digging.

Mighty movers

Too **big** and heavy to use on roads, this giant dump truck is only found in quarries or **mines**, where it carries and **dumps** huge amounts of dirt and rocks.

Hopper
When raised, the top of this hopper is taller than a house, and when the hopper is full, the load weighs more than a jumbo jet!

Load it up
Once an excavator is finished digging, it will clear away the rubble by loading it into a dump truck.

Whooooosh!

Liquid motion

Liquid pumped into hydraulic cylinders makes them extend just like telescopes, raising the hopper.

Hydraulic cylinders

Three for one!

A backhoe loader is a **tractor**, **loader**, and **backhoe** rolled into one. It's small, versatile, quick on its wheels, and very strong.

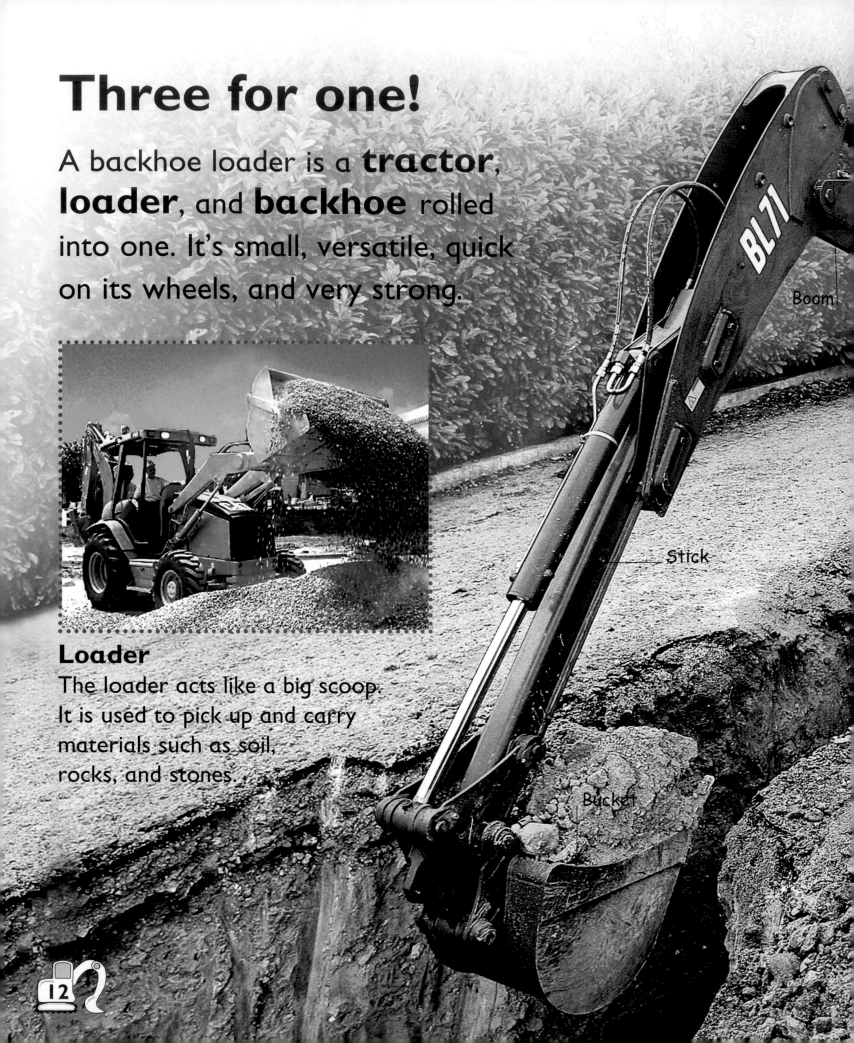

Boom

Stick

Bucket

Loader
The loader acts like a big scoop. It is used to pick up and carry materials such as soil, rocks, and stones.

Backhoe

The backhoe is the main tool and is used for digging and lifting heavy loads. It comes in three parts: boom, stick, and bucket.

Stabilizer legs stop this machine from bouncing around or tipping over while digging.

Loader   Tractor   Backhoe

Tractor

Just like a farm tractor, this backhoe loader has a powerful engine, big, tough tyres, and a cab with steering controls.

A log load

This powerful wheel loader is carrying whole **tree trunks** inside its log-grab attachment. It will carry this heavy load to a nearby sawmill.

Scoop, carry, dump

Wheel loaders are used to pick up earth, rocks, and rubble. They then empty their load into the back of a dump truck, which carries it away.

Log-grab attachment

Wheel care

A machine's wheels must be kept in good repair. The driver must check that the tire treads are undamaged and that the air pressure is correct.

Tree treasures

The wood from these logs can be used to make house frames, tables and chairs, or even the paper you write on!

The engine is in the back, which leaves the front free for attachments.

All change!

Can one machine alone dig, carry, crush, drill, and grip? Yes, if it uses different **attachments**, which are easily removed and replaced.

Snap!

Spring clean

With their powerful jaws and sharp teeth, these tough powerclaws can pick up and clear away debris fast.

Steel teeth

Shaker bucket: used to separate a variety of mixed materials.

Grapple: used to grasp and lift objects such as this rusty piece of scrap metal.

Clamshell: used to carry loose material such as stones or vegetables.

Snap!

Break it up

This excavator is equipped with a breaker. By using this attachment, the operator can drill lots of big holes into a concrete floor.

The more holes drilled, the quicker the concrete will crack and break into pieces.

In a spin

The enormous **drum** on this concrete mixer turns constantly to prevent the wet **concrete** inside from setting and becoming unusable.

Chute

Made by hand

Small cement mixers do much the same job as the large industrial concrete mixers. However, it's a worker who loads the raw materials into the drum, and not machines.

Drum

Firm foundations

By using a vibrator, this worker can break up the thick, sticky concrete that has been poured in, allowing it to flow more easily into the gaps.

Mixed delivery

The drum turns one way to mix the concrete, and the other way to empty it out. The wet concrete comes out of the drum and pours down the chute.

It's a fact

Wet concrete is acidic and can burn if it stays in contact with your skin.

The driver can operate the drum by remote control.

Concrete is a mixture of sand, small stones, cement, and water.

Road recipe

Making a **road** is noisy, dusty, hot, and steamy. Machines must dig, carry, scrape, push, and spread before a road is ready for you to **drive** on!

Blade

Smooth operator
Before a road can be laid, the ground must be made smooth. The top, bumpy layer is scraped off by this grader's metal blade.

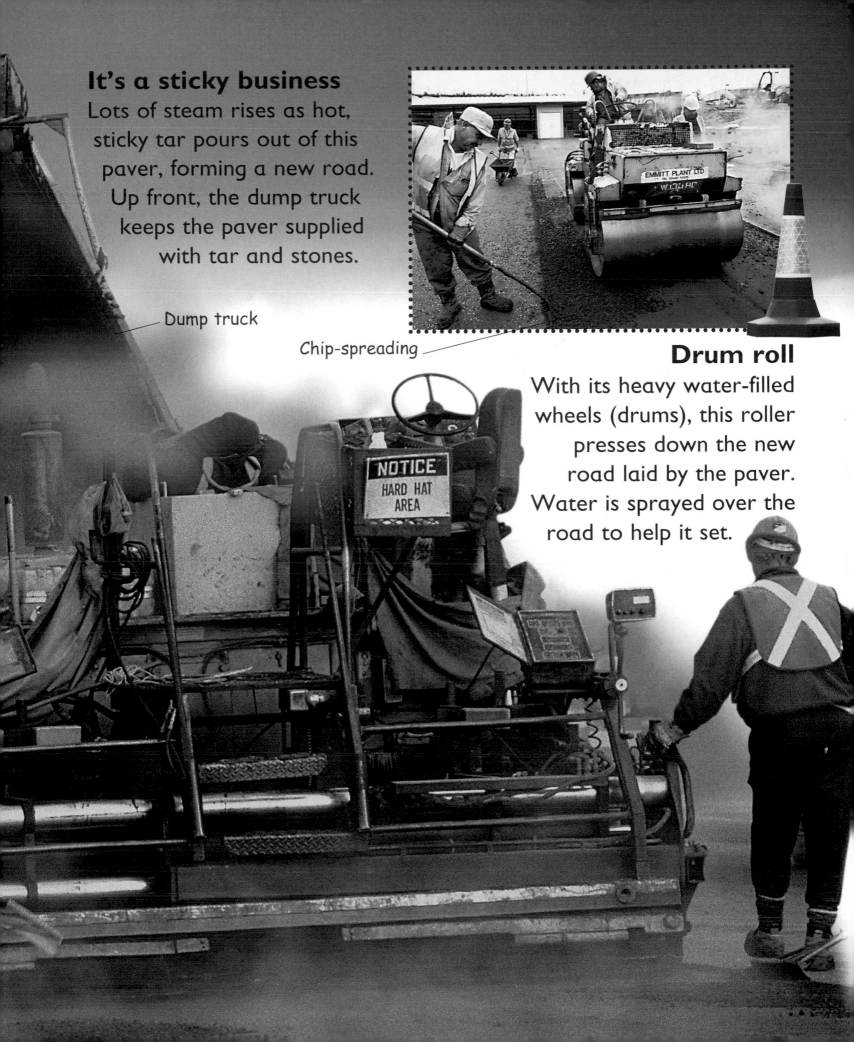

It's a sticky business

Lots of steam rises as hot, sticky tar pours out of this paver, forming a new road. Up front, the dump truck keeps the paver supplied with tar and stones.

Dump truck

Chip-spreading

Drum roll

With its heavy water-filled wheels (drums), this roller presses down the new road laid by the paver. Water is sprayed over the road to help it set.

NOTICE
HARD HAT AREA

Little lifters

These machines are an ideal size to zip in and out of **narrow** spaces, carrying loads in a warehouse, busy city, or on a building site.

Keep it clean
A diesel-run engine can produce soot that would dirty these paper rolls. Therefore, this forklift is powered by gas.

Gas cylinder

Spinning wheel
The wheels on a skid steer can spin in opposite directions allowing the driver to turn around in the smallest possible area.

Higher...higher...higher...higher...higher...stop!

A cherry picker has a sturdy work platform.

Paper roll-clamp attachment

Going up
Cherry pickers are useful for all sorts of tasks, from repairing streetlamps to painting ships.

Sky-high

Cranes are the tallest machines in the world. They reach high into the sky and can lift massive loads, from huge metal beams to whole boats!

On the move
Installed on a special truck, this mobile crane can be driven from site to site. Its arm extends like a telescope.

Jib

This is a small gas-production platform.

Floating cranes
Off-shore drilling stations are built with the help of special cranes that are placed on a huge boat (barge).

Operator's cab

Bird's-eye view

From a small cab far above the city skyline, the operator can control the arm movements of this towering crane.

Tower

Crane barge

Mechanical mole

With its huge spinning **head** and razor-sharp **teeth**, this massive tunnel-boring machine can **cut** through earth, under a seabed, or even through a mountain!

Cutting head

TML 430 T

It's a fact

This amazing machine cleans up after itself, removing rubble with an internal conveyor belt. All that is left behind is a smooth, clean tunnel, ready for development.

It's a heavyweight

A powerful crane is needed to lift this boring machine into place, since it weighs more than 300 cars!

Rocky road

Fitted with 48 tough cutter discs, this huge cutter head can slice through solid rock.

This machine is longer than a football field!

whirr....whirr....whirr....whirr....whirr

Sea trains

Far below the sea, this tunnel-boring machine is busy digging beneath the seabed, making tunnels that will be used by trains.

Days of old

Some of the amazing **machines** you see today weren't around years ago—**people** did the work instead!

Many hands make light work

Teamwork was important, and everyone had specific jobs to do. It took a lot of people-power to make just one building—look at all these workers!

Using a broom attachment, a skid steer can sweep up to 10 times faster than you could!

A big bulldozer could shovel more dirt in just a few seconds than you could in a whole week!

Hook block

Steamy days

This old roller is powered by a steam engine. It uses steam, produced by heat and water, to turn the wheels (drums).

Hanging out

To avoid accidents on building sites today, workers must follow strict safety regulations. You would never see a person taking a ride on a crane today!

Picture gallery

Wheel loader

Some wheel loaders have metal wheel covers that protect the wheels from sharp rocks and stones.

Forklift

Just like the big machines, forklifts must use flashing hazard lights to warn people that they are nearby.

Roller

There are plugs on each roller drum that allow water to be added or removed.

Crane

A computer works out how much a crane can lift at different points along its arm (jib).

Concrete mixer

A mixer's drum must be cleaned out after use to avoid a buildup of hard concrete.

Backhoe loader

The backhoe loader is the most useful machine on a small building site, since it has tools at the front and back.

Excavator

An excavator can dig on one side and dump on the other because its top half spins all the way around.

Attachments

Some machines have more than 13 different kinds of attachments that they can use.

Dump truck

Giant dump trucks are moved from site to site in pieces because they are too big to travel on roads.

Bulldozer

If a machine gets stuck in the mud, a bulldozer can be used to help dig it out or push it clear.

Glossary

Articulated arm has two or more parts connected by joints.

Boom the back part of a machine's arm.

Bucket the scoop of a digging machine.

Counterbalance a static weight that balances a lifted weight.

Chute a channel that directs loose material.

Drum a hollow, barrel-shaped container filled with liquid, such as water.

Demolition the controlled destruction of buildings.

Diesel a fuel used to power engines.

Explosive a material that blows up when lit by an electrical current.

Hydraulic the movement of machine parts that is powered by a liquid, such as oil.

Hopper a container for carrying heavy loads.

Load the material carried by machines.

Engine a machine that burns fuel to make a vehicle work.

Jib the horizontal part of a machine's arm.

Stabilizers the steel legs that stop a stationary vehicle from tipping over.

Stick the first part of a machine's arm just behind the attachment.

Tar a thick, black material used for road-building.

Index

Mining excavator

Acknowledgements

Dorling Kindersley would like to thank Squibb and Davies (Demolition) Ltd, Volvo Construction Equipment Ltd, CNH France, Controlled Demolition Ltd, Komatsu UK, National Maritime Museum, London, Finning (UK) Ltd Caterpillar, and Barloworld Handling Ltd.

Picture credits: